DK

ANNABEL KARMEL

Cook It Together

Find out what we're making on page 16.

LONDON, NEW YORK,
MELBOURNE, MUNICH, and DELHI

Designed by Rachael Foster
Edited by Penny Smith
Design assistance and illustrations
Clémence de Molliens
Photography Dave King
Food stylist Valerie Berry
US Editor Margaret Parrish

Production editor Siu Chan
Jacket editor Mariza O'Keefe
Publishing manager Bridget Giles

First published in the United States in 2009 by
DK Publishing
375 Hudson Street, New York, New York 10014

A catalog record for this book is available
from the Library of Congress

ISBN: 978-0-75664-302-7

Printed and bound by Toppan, China

Discover more at
www.dk.com

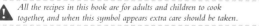
All the recipes in this book are for adults and children to cook
together, and when this symbol appears extra care should be taken.

Contents

Staying cozy indoors and cooking delicious homemade food together is a wonderful way to enjoy your day. So I've created some easy, yet very tasty, step-by-step recipes you and your child will love making together.

Throughout this book, I've focused on 10 important ingredients—tomatoes, corn, potatoes, rice, bananas, strawberries, apples, honey, chocolate, and yogurt. You'll see how they are grown or made and discover fun facts about them.

And I've used lots of wonderful herbs and spices to flavor my recipes. Find out about them on the following page.

Cooking is great for boosting your child's confidence and inspiring creativity. And you never know, you might ignite a passion for cooking in your little ones that goes way beyond licking the spoon: from child cook to Michelin Star chef, perhaps!

So, put on your apron, roll up your sleeves, and get busy!

Annabel Karmel

Fantastic Flavors

Herbs and spices are a wonderful way to add flavor and color to dishes. Here are the ones I've used in recipes in this book.

Sniff

You can buy pots of herbs in supermarkets. They have a wonderful color and smell.

Keeping fresh

Keep dried herbs and spices fresh by storing them in airtight containers in a cool, dark place.

cinnamon

ground cinnamon

cinnamon sticks

This spice is made from the bark of the cinnamon tree, and you buy it as short sticks or powder.

vanilla

vanilla pods

vanilla extract

Vanilla comes from the pod of the vanilla orchid. Use the seeds inside whole pods or vanilla extract.

paprika

This is a fine red spice made from sweet pepper pods. Paprika has a mildly hot flavor.

thyme

A little thyme adds gorgeous flavor to a dish.

mint

Strong and fresh tasting, mint is lovely served with something cooling, such as yogurt.

lemon grass

dill

Dill has a light aniseed flavor.

basil

Basil is lovely with tomatoes.

chives

Chives are from the onion family.

4

ground ginger

To make this bumpy spice easy to grate, try freezing it first.

root ginger

black pepper

Spicy black peppercorns are actually the dried fruit of a kind of vine.

Two types of parsley are often sold in supermarkets.

flat-leaf parsley

cilantro

curly parsley

This looks a little like flat-leaf parsley.

You can grow all kinds of herbs in pots at home. Here's how to grow parsley.

Grow your own parsley

1 First, fill a pot with rich potting soil. Sprinkle over about 5 seeds and cover them with a light layer of soil.

2 Water your seeds well. Keep them on a sunny windowsill. It will take about 8 weeks for them to grow.

3 When the plants are about 3 in (8 cm) tall, carefully dig them out of their first pot...

4 ... and plant them in their own individual pots. You can keep them outside now.

5 Water your parsley regularly and feed it with liquid plant food once a month.

6 When it is dark green and bushy, snip off bits to use in your cooking.

Tomatoes are planted in a freshly plowed field. They need sunshine and plenty of water to grow.

On this plant, unripe tomatoes are yellow. They turn orange, then ripe red.

In cooler climates, tomatoes are grown under cover. They are harvested as soon as they are ripe.

Tomatoes

Tomatoes are actually a fruit, not a vegetable. They are fantastically useful and go in all kinds of things, from bottles of tomato ketchup to salads and soups.

seed

seedling

Grow your own tomatoes

First push a seed into a pot of soil and cover it over. Water it well, and keep it on a sunny windowsill. Your plant will sprout, then grow taller. After about 20 weeks, fruit will form. When the tomatoes are ripe, pick them and enjoy!

It takes 25 tomatoes to fill one bottle of ketchup.

beef tomato

Tomatoes will not ripen in the fridge because it is too cold. So keep them at room temperature for the best color and flavor.

plum tomato

baby cherry tomato

baby plum tomato

regular tomato

cherry tomato

Tomatoes are usually red but some varieties are yellow or purple.

Tomatoes can be as small as a grape, as big as a melon, or any size in between.

Tomato Bruschetta

Bruschetta is Italian for toast, and these warm, juicy tomatoes on toast make a lovely lunch or light supper.

You will need:
1 heaping cup (240 g) cherry tomatoes (that's about 20)
2½ tsp olive oil
4 small sprigs thyme
salt and pepper
4 slices country-style bread
1 clove garlic
basil leaves
Parmesan

Halve

Scatter

Rub

1 Preheat the oven to 400°F (200°C). Line a baking sheet with baking parchment. Halve the tomatoes and sit them on the baking sheet.

2 Drizzle over 1 tsp of the olive oil and scatter over the thyme leaves. Season with salt and pepper. Bake the tomatoes for 6–8 minutes until soft.

3 Toast the bread and let it cool a little. Cut the garlic in half and rub it over one side of the toast. Trickle on the remaining olive oil.

Makes 4

cherry tomatoes

4 Carefully spoon the tomatoes onto the toast and scatter over the basil leaves. Use a potato peeler to shave a few flakes of Parmesan on top. Serve warm.

7

Tomato Soup

Serves 4

This is tomato soup with a smile. It makes a delicious light meal when served with crispy bread or breadsticks.

You will need:

1 small red onion
½ small red pepper
½ carrot
1 clove garlic
1 tbsp olive oil
14½ oz (400 g) can chopped tomatoes
3 tbsp tomato puree
3 tbsp tomato ketchup
2 tbsp sugar
small bunch fresh thyme leaves
1 cup (250 ml) vegetable stock
salt and pepper
4 tbsp heavy cream
basil leaves, olive slices, whipped cream, to serve

Chop

1 First prepare the vegetables: chop the onion and dice the pepper into large chunks.

Crush

2 Peel the carrot, then grate it on the roughest side of the grater. Crush the garlic.

3 Heat the oil, add the onion, pepper, and carrot, and cook for 5 minutes. Pour in the canned tomatoes, and add the tomato puree, tomato ketchup, garlic, sugar, thyme, and stock. Simmer for 30 minutes.

Pour

☆**Annabel's Tip**
Use thyme leaves, not stalk. Somewhere around 10 leaves is about right.

4 Season the mixture with salt and pepper. Then blend the soup until it's smooth. Stir in the 4 tbsp cream and serve.

Blend

☆ **Annabel's Tip**

To decorate your soup with funny faces, make eyes from basil leaves and olive slices, then pipe on the rest of the faces using whipped cream. And remember, the cooler the soup, the longer your faces will stay put!

ears of corn ready for picking

Corn

Corn is a high-energy food that is healthy and delicious. You can buy it fresh, still wrapped in its green leaves, or canned, or frozen, or dried. The best fresh corn has plump kernels full of sweet, milky juice.

Corn is similar to maize. It grows in warm places. Most of the world's corn comes from the US.

corn on the cob

kernels

There are about 600–800 kernels on an average corn on the cob.

Count the rows on a piece of corn. How many are there? The answer is always an even number.

silks

The tufted parts on an ear of corn are called silks. They turn brown at the ends when the corn is ready to pick.

The ear is covered by tightly wrapped leaves called the husk.

These dried corn kernels are used to make popcorn.

popping corn

POP!

From this... ...to this

mini sweetcorn

Put the dried corn kernels in a pan with a little oil and they will pop into POPCORN!

Corn and Chicken
Pasta Salad

Corn, chicken, and noodles
are often seen together in soups,
but here is something similar
as a yummy salad.

You will need:

8 oz (225 g) bow tie pasta
6 oz (150 g) cooked chicken
4 scallions
1 large tomato
2 tbsp mayonnaise
2 tbsp Greek yogurt
½ tsp lemon juice
2-3 sprigs dill
salt and pepper
1¼ cup (198 g) corn, drained

Deseed

1 Cook the pasta
according to the
instructions on the
package. Rinse with
cold water. Then
shred the chicken,
slice the scallions,
deseed and chop
the tomato.

2 Put the
mayonnaise,
yogurt, and lemon
juice in a large
bowl. Snip in the dill,
season with salt and
pepper, and then stir
everything together.

Snip

3 Now pour the
cold pasta,
chicken, scallions,
chopped tomato,
and corn onto the
mayonnaise mixture.

Pour

4 Mix all the
ingredients
together and serve.

Mix

11

Corn Fritters

These are popular in the South and are great eaten with friends and family. For big parties, simply double the quantities!

You will need:

¼ cup (30 g) flour
1 tsp baking powder
pinch of salt
1 egg
1 tbsp maple syrup
2 tbsp milk
1¼ cup (200 g) corn, drained
2 scallions, chopped
1-2 tbsp sunflower oil
tomatoes and basil, to serve

Sift

1 First sift the flour, baking powder, and pinch of salt into a large bowl.

Pour

2 Separate the egg by pouring the yolk from one half of the shell to the other. Let the egg white fall into one bowl. Drop the yolk into another.

Pour

3 Add the maple syrup and milk to the egg yolk and whisk together. Pour this mixture over the flour. Stir everything together to make a batter.

Whisk

4 Then whisk the egg white until it forms stiff peaks. Be careful not to overwhisk or it will go flat.

Fold

5 Use a spatula to fold the egg white into the flour mixture—carefully stirring around the side of the bowl and across the middle.

6 Next pour the corn and chopped scallions into the batter mixture. Fold them in—be as light as you can here.

7 Heat the oil, drop in tablespoons of the batter and cook for 1-2 minutes until the undersides are golden. Flip over, cook the other sides, then serve.

These fritters are delicious served with a **tomato** and **basil salad**.

juicy pieces of corn

Makes 8-10

☆Annabel's Tip
Try dishing up these fritters for breakfast. Simply serve them with chopped banana and extra maple syrup.

To make the field ready for planting, the farmer plows the soil and lifts out any stones. Then he uses a potato-planting machine to drop seed potatoes into the soil and cover them over.

Around 2-6 weeks after planting, the shoots begin to push out of the soil. Under the ground, potatoes (called tubers) form. Once the plants flower, young new potatoes can be harvested.

At the end of the summer, mature potatoes are ready to be dug up. These can be stored for months—but make sure you keep them in the dark since light makes them turn green.

Potatoes

People have been growing potatoes for centuries. And whatever their color—white, brown, yellow, purple, red, or blue—potatoes are a delicious and filling addition to any meal.

You can do lots of things with potatoes, you can...

roast them
boil them
mash them
fry them
bake them

Potatoes were the first food ever to be grown in orbit. In 1995 potato leaves taken on board Space Shuttle Columbia sprouted tubers.

Potatoes are sliced and cooked in oil to make delicious chips.

Potatoes can turn into new potato plants when they sprout green shoots.

white potato

sweet potato

Potatoes have thin skins. Their flesh is usually white.

baby or new potatoes

These are orange inside.

Potato Wedges

These wedges are a healthy and easy alternative to fries, but just as delicious. You can make them spicy by adding paprika or fajita seasoning.

You will need:

2 large potatoes
1 tbsp olive oil
salt and pepper
½ tsp paprika or fajita seasoning (optional)

Sour cream dip

Mix together 3 tbsp sour cream, 1 tbsp mayonnaise, 2 tsp milk, 2 tsp snipped chives, and ½ crushed clove garlic. Season with salt and pepper and serve with the wedges.

Serve with a sour cream and chive dip.

Cut

1 Preheat the oven to 400°F (200°C). Cut each potato lengthwise into thick wedges.

Mix

2 Put the oil, salt, and pepper into a bowl. Add the paprika or fajita seasoning, if using. Then add the potatoes and mix thoroughly.

Bake

Bake the wedges for 30 minutes, turning 2 or 3 times during cooking. They'll be tasty and golden when they're cooked.

3 Lay the wedges on a baking sheet lined with parchment.

Potato Soufflés

Makes 4

The word *soufflé* comes from the French *souffler*, which means "to puff." When you see these come out of the oven, you'll understand why!

You will need:

¼ stick (30 g) butter,
   plus extra for greasing
3 oz (85 g) aged Cheddar
1 oz (30 g) Parmesan
small bunch chives
2 eggs
1 large baking potato, cooked
6 tbsp milk
pepper

Butter

⚠

1 Preheat the oven to 450°F (220°C) and put a baking sheet in the oven to heat up. Then generously butter 4 ramekin dishes.

Grate

⚠

2 Grate the Cheddar and Parmesan cheeses. Snip the chives into small pieces (you should have about 2 tsp). Then separate the eggs.

⚠

Cook your potato

You can microwave your potato for 7-8 minutes. Alternatively, boil it whole and unpeeled for 35 minutes or until tender. Peel when cool.

Annabel's Tip

Soufflés don't stay risen for very long, so it is best to get everyone ready to eat before you take them out of the oven. Serve right away (though be careful since they will be hot!).

3 Put the potato flesh in a bowl and mash well. Then stir in the cheeses, chives, and egg yolks.

Mash

Fill

6 Fill the prepared ramekins with the mixture. Put the ramekins on the hot baking sheet and bake for 15–17 minutes until puffed and golden.

Pour

⚠️

4 Warm the milk and butter in a pan, then pour this over the potato mixture and stir everything together. Season with pepper (the Parmesan is already salty).

Whisk

5 Whisk the egg whites to floppy peaks. Next gently fold the egg whites into the potato mixture.

Rice is grown in flooded meadows called paddies. The water helps to keep away weeds.

After about 4 months, rice is ready for harvesting. It is picked by hand or combine harvester.

This field has been partly harvested. The hard rice grains are carried away in bags.

Rice

Rice is an excellent pantry ingredient because it keeps for ages and has a mild flavor that goes with lots of food. A little rice goes a long way—when you cook it, it swells to three times is original size.

There are around 40,000 types of rice, although only a small number of them are sold in our supermarkets.

Rice has two outer layers, like coats. On the outside is the hull, under this is the bran, and under this, a grain of white rice.

• Rice is the main food for half the people in the world—in Asia, many eat it for breakfast, lunch, and dinner.

• Rice is easy to digest, so it is one of the first foods given to babies.

• Puffed rice cereal is made from rice that has been popped—a little like popcorn.

When rice is cooked it can be **fluffy** or **sticky**.

brown rice

Brown rice still has its bran layer. It tastes nutty.

short grain rice

This type of rice is light and fluffy when cooked.

long grain rice

arborio short grain rice

Short grain rice is good to eat with chopsticks because the grains are soft and stick together.

A creamy rice, arborio is excellent at soaking up flavors.

Arancini

These rice balls with melted cheese centers are delicious. Serve with a ready-made tomato sauce or make your own (see below).

Cook

Makes 5 large balls

Tomato sauce
Heat 1 tbsp olive oil and cook 1 diced shallot and 1 crushed clove garlic. Add 14½ oz (400 g) can tomatoes, 1 tsp brown sugar, and 1 tbsp ketchup. Cook for 15 minutes.

You will need:
1 tsp olive oil
1 tbsp diced onion
⅓ cup (60 g) risotto rice
1 cup (250 ml) chicken or vegetable stock
3 tbsp grated Parmesan
salt and pepper
5½ oz (150 g) mozzarella, cut into 5 x ¾ in (1½ cm) cubes
2 tbsp dried breadcrumbs
1 egg, beaten with a pinch of salt
oil, for frying

These are made with **risotto rice** *and stick together perfectly!*

runny **mozzarella middles**

1 Heat the oil. Cook the onion. Add rice and stock. Simmer for 25 minutes until cooked, stirring often. Add 2 tbsp Parmesan, salt and pepper.

2 Cool then refrigerate the rice for 3 hours or until firm. Then break it up, divide it into 5 portions, and squash into balls.

Squash

3 Make a hole in each ball and push in a piece of mozzarella. Squish the rice around the cheese.

Squish

4 Mix the breadcrumbs with the remaining Parmesan. Dip the rice balls in the egg.

Dip

5 Roll the rice balls in the breadcrumb mix.

Roll

6 When the balls are completely coated, fry them in oil for 5 minutes or until golden.

Coated!

19

Paella

Paella was first made in Spain and gets its name from the pan it was cooked in—a *paellera*. This is a *paella mixta*, using seafood and chicken.

You will need:

1 onion
½ red pepper
1 clove garlic
1 tbsp olive oil
1 tsp smoked paprika or
    ordinary paprika
1¼ cup (200 g) long grain rice
2½ cup (600 ml) chicken stock
2 tbsp tomato puree
6 oz (170 g) cooked chicken
handful parsley leaves
⅓ cup (60 g) frozen peas
6 oz (170 g) cooked jumbo shrimp

Cooking with garlic

Choose plump garlic, and peel off the papery covering before chopping or squeezing in a garlic press.

Squeeze

Cook

1 First, finely chop the onion, dice the pepper, and crush the garlic.

2 Heat the oil in a large nonstick frying pan and cook the onion for 5 minutes until soft.

3 Then add the pepper, garlic, and paprika. Pour in the rice and cook everything for 3 minutes, stirring constantly.

Pour

4 Next, mix together the stock and tomato puree and pour this onto the rice mixture. Simmer for around 15 minutes until the rice is tender and the stock is absorbed. If the rice becomes too dry, add a little water.

Pour

Annabel's Tip

If you want an even more tomato-ey paella, try reducing the stock to ⅞ cup (200 ml) and adding a can of chopped tomatoes with the other ingredients at step 4.

5 While the rice is cooking, shred the chicken into small pieces and roughly chop the parsley leaves.

Shred

Add

6 Add the peas, shrimp, and chicken to the paella and cook for a further 2 minutes, until everything is hot. Scatter over the chopped parsley and serve.

The banana plant reaches its full height of 15-30 ft (4-9 m) in about one year.

Each banana plant produces just one stem of fruit. Farmers cover it in plastic to stop insects from laying their eggs in the fruit.

Bananas are harvested while they are still green. The heavy fruit is hung on cables so it can be moved around easily without bruising.

Bananas grow UPward.

Bananas

This popular, peelable fruit only grows in hot, tropical places. It is harvested all year round—so there are usually lots of bananas available in our supermarkets.

This is a banana flower. In some countries, it is eaten as a vegetable.

India is by far the largest producer of bananas in the world. There the banana flower is thought to bring good luck.

Monkeys like bananas too!

Some monkeys open bananas from the opposite end from us, pinching it with their fingers and tearing it open. Others eat the skin, too!

At the factory, the bananas are cut into bunches of around 6-8 bananas. These are washed and cooled in big baths of water.

types of bananas

baby banana

red banana

regular banana

plantain

Bananas are full of starch. This turns to sugar as the banana ripens, making it taste sweet.

The bananas are checked for unwanted insects. They are weighed, labeled, packed in boxes, and sent to stores all around the world.

ready to eat

Chop

Melt

Drizzle

Roll

Banana Bites

This light dessert is fun for children to make. It works best with slightly underripe bananas.

You will need:

1–2 bananas
4 oz (110 g) chocolate—milk or plain
dried coconut
sprinkles

Makes 6

1 Peel the banana and trim off the ends. Chop the flesh into 6 pieces.

2 Break the chocolate into a heatproof bowl. Put the bowl over a pan of hot water to melt the chocolate, stirring occasionally. Leave to cool slightly.

3 Push a straw through the banana, then drizzle melted chocolate over each piece. (Don't worry if it's not perfect—it will still taste delicious!)

4 Roll the chocolate-covered banana in the coconut or sprinkles. Let the chocolate harden, then serve.

chocolate sprinkles

coconut

colored sprinkles

23

Banana Butterfly Cakes

Makes 8

These little cakes can be eaten plain, or covered in my sweet and sticky caramel topping—they'll be a family favorite!

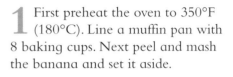

Mash

1 First preheat the oven to 350°F (180°C). Line a muffin pan with 8 baking cups. Next peel and mash the banana and set it aside.

You will need:

For the cakes
- 1 large banana
- 1 stick (110 g) butter
- ½ cup (110 g) sugar
- 2 eggs
- ¾ tsp vanilla extract
- ⅞ cup (110 g) self-rising flour

For the icing
- 3 oz (85 g) cream cheese
- 3 tsp (40 g) unsalted butter
- ⅓ cup (85 g) Dulche de Leche
- ⅓ cup (40 g) powdered sugar, plus extra for dusting

☆Annabel's Tip
You can use any size nozzle to pipe the icing. I've used a fairly large one so the icing squeezes out easily.

☆Annabel's Tip
Dulche de Leche is a kind of caramel that you can buy in many supermarkets. It's a perfect ingredient for the caramel topping on these cakes.

Beat

2 Put the butter and sugar in a large bowl and beat until pale and fluffy. In a separate bowl, beat together the eggs and vanilla. Then add the eggs to the butter mixture, a little at a time, beating thoroughly.

24

Sift

Fill

Beat

3 Now add the banana to the butter mixture and stir it in. Then sift the flour over the top and fold it in.

4 Fill the baking cups with the mixture. Bake for 20 minutes, or until risen and springy to the touch.

5 To make the icing, beat together the cream cheese and butter. Then beat in the Dulche de Leche and sugar.

Pipe

6 Slice the tops off the cakes and cut the tops in half to make butterfly wings. Pipe or spoon the icing onto each cake. Dust the wings with powdered sugar, pop them on the cakes and serve.

☆Annabel's Tip
If you like, you can pipe a butterfly shape onto each cake using melted chocolate or writing icing.

Strawberries grow best in warm, sunny places. Farmers put straw under the plants to keep the fruit dry and protect it from rotting.

A strawberry flower has five white petals and a bright yellow center. This is where the strawberry fruit grows, as the petals fall away.

Strawberries only ripen when they are on the plant, so pick them when they are plump and red. If you pick them green, they stay green!

Strawberries

I love the beautiful red color, melting texture, and sweet flavor of strawberries! They're a hugely popular fruit, and each year over two million tons of them are grown in gardens and fields around the world.

Farmers have found ways to grow the fruit all year long. This polytunnel works like a giant greenhouse. Sunlight gets in, but cold weather doesn't.

First comes the flower.

The petals fall off...

...as the fruit appears.

It gets bigger...

...and BIGGER.

Strawberries are the only fruit that have seeds on the outside.

Each strawberry has around 200 seeds.

Strawberry Layers

This is a supereasy recipe that can be used to make a rich layered dessert or breakfast treat, or around eight perfect ice pops.

You will need:

2⅓ cups (350 g) whole strawberries
4 tbsp strawberry jam
⅞ cup (200 ml) heavy cream
6 tbsp Greek yogurt
mint, to serve

☆ Annabel's Tip
For delicious ice pops, simply stir together the strawberry and cream mixtures, put in molds, and freeze.

Serves 6

1 Destem the strawberries. Put a few aside for decoration and slice the rest into a bowl with the jam.

2 Use a potato masher to mash up the strawberries and jam.

3 In a separate bowl, whisk the cream to stiff peaks. Then fold the yogurt into the cream.

4 Layer the strawberry and cream mixtures in little serving dishes.

Decorate with strawberries and mint.

Destem

Mash

Whisk

Strawberry Cheesecakes

These little cheesecakes are lovely made in heart-shaped pans, but the ingredients work just as well as one larger cheesecake, cut into slices.

Crush

Pour

Press

You will need:

sunflower oil, for greasing

6 oz (170 g) graham crackers

¾ stick (85 g) butter

1 cup (150 g) whole strawberries, plus extra to decorate

⅛ cup (30 g) sugar

2 tbsp water

1 package (3 oz/85 g) strawberry gelatin

7 oz (200 g) cream cheese

⅞ cup (200 ml) whipping cream

1 Grease cake pans with sunflower oil. Put graham crackers in a plastic bag and crush into fine crumbs using a rolling pin. Pour into a bowl. Melt the butter, pour it onto the cracker crumbs, and mix thoroughly. Press into the bottoms of the pans.

☆ **Annabel's Tip**

To make one big cheesecake, use a loose-bottomed cake pan that's about 8 in (20 cm) across.

Decorate with strawberries before serving.

Chop

Slide

Pour

2 Next chop the strawberries into smallish pieces.

3 Slide them into a pan. Add the sugar and water and simmer until the strawberries are soft. Remove from the heat, add the gelatin, and stir until smooth.

4 Leave the strawberry mixture to cool. Whip the cream cheese. Pour the strawberry mixture onto the cheese.

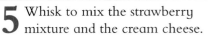
Whisk

Spoon

Smooth

5 Whisk to mix the strawberry mixture and the cream cheese.

6 Whisk the cream to stiff peaks. Spoon it onto the strawberry and cream cheese mixture and fold in. (It will start to set.)

7 Spoon the creamy mixture onto the crackers in the pans. Smooth out the tops and refrigerate for 2 hours until set.

Apple trees in spring
This is when blossom grows on the trees. Flowers are pink, then gradually turn white. Bees pollinate the flowers so fruit can form.

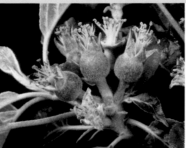

Apple trees in summer
When the blossom falls, apples begin to grow in its place. They grow big and round and ripen in the sunshine.

Apple trees in the fall
The apples are ready! They are picked by hand so they don't get bruised. Then they are sent to groceries and markets for sale.

Apples

Apples are a fantastic fruit as they are equally delicious in savory and sweet dishes. They've been grown for around 4,000 years and are one of the oldest and best-liked fruits there is.

I'm top seed!

There are all sorts of *varieties* of apples. Here are a few of them.

There are nearly 10,000 different varieties of apple.

Apple trees can keep on producing fruit for over 100 years.

The country that produces the most apples each year is China.

Royal Gala

Bramley

Tentation

Golden Delicious

Braeburn

Pink Lady

Red Delicious

Much of an apple's goodness is just under the skin, so don't peel it before you eat it!

To stop a cut apple from turning brown, sprinkle it with lemon juice.

About a quarter of an apple is air. That's why it floats!

Baked Apples

Eating or cooking apples are equally good in this super-simple recipe. It's delicious served with my sauce suggestion below, or with a lovely big dollop of yogurt!

You will need:

4 apples
6 tbsp raisins
3 tbsp brown sugar
¼ tsp cinnamon
1 tsp (15 g) butter
6 tbsp water

Core

Stuff

Pour

1 Preheat the oven to 350°F (180°C). Remove the cores from the apples using an apple corer. Then put the apples in a baking dish.

2 Mix together the raisins, brown sugar, and cinnamon. Stuff this mixture into the holes in the apples. Top with the butter.

3 Pour about 6 tbsp water around the apples so it just covers the bottom of the dish. Bake for 35-40 minutes, basting halfway through cooking.

Serves 4

*Before cooking, **score** around the apples so they don't **burst open**.*

☆ Annabel's Tip
For a quick-and-easy treat, serve each apple with 1 tbsp Dulche de Leche mixed with a little cream.

31

Apple Meringue Tarts

These simple little apple tarts topped with meringue are tasty eaten warm or cold. Serve them with vanilla yogurt or cream.

You will need:

For the tarts

7 oz (200 g) ready-made pastry crust
2-3 apples
2 tbsp water
1 tbsp (15 g) sugar
1 tsp lemon juice

For the meringue

1 large egg white
3 tbsp (40 g) superfine sugar

The meringue should be soft on the inside...

...and slightly crisp on the outside.

☆ **Annabel's Tip**
If you have any cooked apple left over, try stirring it into plain yogurt for a delicious breakfast treat.

Cut

Use a 3½ in
(8½ cm) cutter.

1 Preheat the oven to 400°F (200°C). Cut 6 circles
from the pastry and use these to line a muffin pan.

Peel

2 Peel, chop, and cook the apples in the water until soft
and fairly dry. Stir in the sugar and lemon juice.

Spoon

3 Let the apples cool a little then mash them into small
pieces. Spoon into the pastry cases and bake in the oven
for 15 minutes.

Whisk

4 For the meringue, whisk the egg to stiff peaks. Whisk in
1 tbsp sugar, then whisk in the remaining sugar. Pipe or
spoon onto the apple and cook for a further 3–5 minutes.

Apple & Chicken Curry

This mildly spicy curry is made with ingredients you can buy at your local supermarket. The apple adds a subtle sweetness to the dish.

You will need:

1 onion
1 clove garlic
3 scallions
1 medium apple
1 tbsp vegetable oil
1–2 tsp mild curry paste
1 tsp soy sauce
⅔ cup (150 ml) coconut milk
1 chicken stock cube, dissolved in
   ⅔ cup (150 ml) boiling water
2 in (5 cm) piece lemongrass
2 chicken breasts, cubed
¾ cup (110 g) frozen peas
salt and pepper
cilantro, sliced lime, and boiled
   jasmine rice, to serve

Serves 4

1 First prepare your vegetables and fruit: peel and chop the onion, crush the garlic. Thinly slice the scallions. Cut the apple into thin slices.

Cut

Pour

☆ Annabel's Tip
To shape your jasmine rice into a star, grease a star-shaped mold with sunflower oil. Spoon cooked rice into the mold. Push it down. Then carefully slip off the mold.

2 Heat the oil in a wok. Add the onion and cook for 5–6 minutes until soft. Add the garlic and curry paste and cook for 1 minute. Then pour in the soy sauce, coconut milk, and chicken stock, stirring constantly.

34

Add apples

Add peas

3 Add the lemongrass, chicken, and apple. Bring the curry to a boil, then reduce the heat and simmer for 6–8 minutes until the chicken has cooked through.

4 Add the peas and scallions and cook for a further 1–2 minutes. Season to taste with salt (the soy sauce is salty so be careful) and pepper.

jasmine rice

slice of apple

5 Remove the lemongrass and spoon the curry onto plates. Serve with a sprinkling of cilantro, a few slices of lime, and boiled rice.

People keep honeybees in wooden hives so that the honey can be collected easily. Fifty thousand bees can live in each hive. These are worker bees, drone bees, and just one queen bee.

Here honey is being scraped off honeycomb. But honeycomb can also be put into a machine that spins very fast so that the honey flies out. Then the honey is put in jars.

Bees make honey from a sweet liquid, called nectar, which they suck out of flowers. Many flowers have bright colors to help bees find the nectar.

When the honey is ready, bee keepers puff smoke into the hives to make the bees sleepy. Then they pull the honeycombs out of the hives. Honeycombs contain the honey.

Honey

Bees make honey to feed themselves during the winter. But they often produce more than they need, so people collect the extra and use it to add a touch of sweetness to all kinds of recipes.

Dip a honey spoon in honey and twirl it around. It picks up lots of honey and drips less than an ordinary spoon.

buzz

• Workers are female bees. Each worker makes around ½ tsp honey in its lifetime.

• The drones are male bees. They fertilize the eggs the queen bee lays.

• The queen is the only bee that can have babies.

Bees fill honeycomb with honey, then cover it over with wax until the honey is needed.

Bees live in hives and in the wild. This nest of wild bees is in Thailand.

Honey can be creamy yellow, golden, or amber.

You can eat honeycomb like this. Not all honey tastes the same. The flavor comes from the flowers the bees feed on.

Salmon Skewers

Here I've used honey and soy sauce to make a type of glaze called teriyaki. It's delicious on salmon.

You will need:

4 tbsp honey
4 tsp soy sauce
2 tsp rice wine vinegar
¼ tsp grated ginger
6 oz (170 g) skinless salmon fillet, cut into cubes
1 tsp water

Decorate with curls of scallion.

Serves 4

First soak 6 wooden skewers in warm water for 30 minutes. Heat the broiler to high.

1 Mix together the honey, soy sauce, and vinegar. Pour half into a pan and set aside. Add ginger to the remaining mixture in the bowl.

2 Pour the ginger mixture onto the salmon. Mix to coat.

3 Thread the salmon onto the skewers, then put them on a foil-lined baking sheet.

Spoon on sauce from the bowl. Broil the salmon for 2–3 minutes on each side or until cooked. Add the water to the sauce in the pan. Simmer for 30 seconds, then serve with the salmon.

☆**Annabel's Tip**
To make the scallions curl, cut them into thin slices and put them in icy cold water.

Add

Pour

Thread

Ready to broil

37

Honey Cakes

Although these little cakes are sweet enough to eat on their own, children love making bees and flowers to decorate them. So help them get busy!

You will need:

For the cakes
½ stick (60 g) butter
¼ cup, packed (60 g) light brown sugar
4 tbsp honey
1 egg
½ tsp vanilla extract
2 tbsp apple puree
⅔ cup (85 g) self-rising flour
½ tsp ground cinnamon
¼ tsp ground ginger

For the bees and flowers
7 oz (200 g) marzipan
melted chocolate or writing icing
12 slivered almonds
sprinkles

Pour

Makes 6

1 Preheat the oven to 350°F (180°C). Line a muffin pan with 6 baking cups. Put the butter and sugar in a mixing bowl. Pour in the honey and beat everything together until fluffy.

Sift

2 In another bowl, beat the egg, vanilla, and apple puree, then beat this into the butter mixture. Sift over the flour, cinnamon, and ginger.

Fold

3 Now fold in the dry ingredients by running your spatula around the outside of the bowl and across the middle until everything is well mixed.

Fill

4 Fill the baking cups with the mixture. Bake for 18–22 minutes, until risen, golden, and firm to the touch. Leave to cool on a wire rack.

Shape

Paint

☆ **Annabel's Tip**
For nut-free decorations, make the bees with yellow-fondant-icing bodies and chocolate-button wings.

5 To make the bees, shape the heads and bodies from marzipan and gently squash them together so they stick. Cut out flower shapes.

6 Paint on the bees' faces and stripes using melted chocolate or writing icing. Push slivered almonds into the sides for wings. Press sprinkles into the flowers.

Cut out the flowers using a cookie cutter.

I've got my stripes!

Decorate your cakes with bees and flowers.

cocoa pod

cocoa beans

white pulp

Cocoa pods grow on the trunk and main branches of a cacoa tree. When the pods are split open, you can see the cocoa beans inside.

Cocoa pods grow to the size of melons. Workers cut them from the trees when they are a ripe yellow to dark red color.

Chocolate

Sweet, creamy, and rich, chocolate is one of my favorite cooking ingredients! It is made from cocoa beans, the seeds of the cacao tree that grow in tropical rain forests.

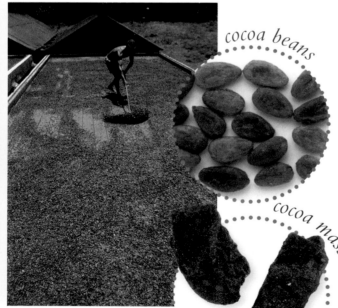

cocoa beans

cocoa mass

cocoa butter

• Here a worker is spreading out wet cocoa beans to dry in the sun.

• Then they're sent to a factory where the shells are removed, leaving the insides, called *nibs*.

• The nibs are roasted, ground, and pressed to separate them into *cocoa mass* and *cocoa butter*.

• The cocoa mass is melted and mixed with sugar and some of the cocoa butter. It's poured into molds and hardened into the chocolate bars we buy in stores.

Chocolate melts at just below body temperature—that's why it turns to liquid so quickly when you hold it in your hand.

Swiss people eat more chocolate per head than any nation on Earth.

PLAIN CHOCOLATE is cocoa mass mixed with sugar and cocoa butter.

MILK CHOCOLATE has the same ingredients as dark chocolate, but also contains milk.

WHITE CHOCOLATE only contains cocoa butter—not cocoa mass. That's why some people don't think it's really chocolate at all.

Chocolate Truffles

Homemade chocolate truffles make delicious gifts.
For a special present, place a few truffles on a piece
of cardboard, wrap in plastic, and tie with ribbon.

You will need:

4 oz (100 g) bar of plain
or milk chocolate
3 tbsp double cream
½ tsp vanilla extract
½ oz (15 g) butter
2 tbsp cocoa powder
2 tbsp coconut

Snap

Stir

Roll

1 Snap the chocolate into a bowl. Add the cream, vanilla, and butter. Put the bowl over a pan of simmering water to melt the chocolate, stirring occasionally.

2 Let the chocolate mixture cool, then put it in the fridge. Stir every 5 minutes or so until the mixture is thick and fudgy.

3 For each truffle, roll a teaspoon of the fudge mixture into a ball in your hands (quickly so it doesn't melt). Then roll it in cocoa powder or coconut.

☆ **Annabel's Tip**
*Lay the truffles on
baking parchment
and store in the fridge
for up to a week—if
they last that long!*

a delicious treat

Makes
12-15

41

Dark and White Chocolate Cakes

Makes 3 (easily doubled)

These rich chocolate cakes hide a surprise— as you cut into them, white chocolate comes flowing out! Serve on special occasions.

You will need:

1 stick (110 g) butter, plus extra
   for greasing
6 oz (150 g) plain chocolate
1 whole egg
2 egg yolks
3 tbsp sugar
½ tsp vanilla extract
1 tbsp cornstarch
3 white chocolate truffles
vanilla ice-cream, to serve

✩Annabel's Tip
You can use white chocolate instead of the truffles. Use 2 squares of chocolate in each cake and cook for at least 14 minutes to give the white chocolate a chance to melt.

Snap

1 Preheat oven to 375°F (190°C). Generously butter 3 metal ramekins and line the bases with circles of baking parchment.

2 Break the chocolate into a heatproof bowl. Add the butter and put the bowl over a saucepan of hot water so the chocolate and butter melt, stirring occasionally. Set aside to cool slightly.

42

Beat

Pour

Place

3 Put the egg, yolks, sugar, and vanilla in a bowl. Using an electric mixer on high, beat them together for 4-6 minutes until pale and about 4 times the original volume.

4 Pour the chocolate mixture into the egg mixture. Add the cornstarch and whisk everything together to make a batter.

5 Spoon 2 tbsp of the batter into each ramekin and place one truffle in each. Cover the truffles with the remaining batter.

6 Put the ramekins on a baking sheet and bake for 10-12 minutes until just set on the surface. Leave for 2 minutes, then turn out onto plates and serve right away with vanilla ice cream.

Sweet treasure hidden here...

Most yogurt is made from cows' milk. Friendly (live) bacteria in the milk make it thicken and take on a tangy, yogurty flavor. One cow produces enough milk in a day to make more than 100 little cups of yogurt.

Yogurt

Yogurt is made from milk. Although you can buy it in supermarkets, it is actually very easy to make yourself. And you can use any milk you like—whole, low-fat, skim, goat's milk, sheep's milk—they all work!

• Yogurt was first eaten over 2,000 years ago. It was probably discovered accidentally when milk was left out in the sun.

• Yogurt is a good source of calcium, so will help build strong bones and teeth.

• Some yogurt contains living bacteria that can help you digest your food.

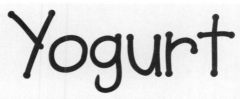

Lots of yogurt has added sugar—this sweetens the flavor and helps the yogurt last.

Homemade yogurt

1 First boil 4 cups (1L) milk to kill unwanted bacteria. Let it cool.

2 Then add a 6 oz (170 g) container of plain yogurt to the milk and stir it in. Choose a yogurt that says "active cultures" on the label.

3 Keep the mixture warm—around 110°F (43°C). You can either put it on a radiator or in a very low oven for 6 hours or overnight.

4 The mixture will thicken and turn to yogurt. You can eat this plain (although it is fairly tart), or add fruit and honey. Enjoy!

☆**Annabel's Tip**
Look out for frozen yogurt in the ice-cream section of your supermarket. It's delicious on chopped-up banana or a bowl of berries.

Fruit Brûlée

Yogurt makes a perfect topping for a fruit brulee. *Brûlée* means "burned" in French, but really the sugar is grilled until it has just melted.

Serves 4

You will need:
1⅓ cup (200 g) whole strawberries
¾ cup (110 g) blueberries
3 tbsp powdered sugar
½ cup (120 ml) heavy cream
7 oz (200 g) Greek yogurt
½ tsp vanilla extract
2 tbsp turbinado (raw) sugar

Dust

Whisk

Spoon

1 Destem and quarter the strawberries and put them into a bowl with the blueberries. Dust over 1 tbsp powdered sugar and toss to coat the berries.

2 Whisk the cream to soft peaks. In a separate bowl, mix together the yogurt, vanilla, and remaining powdered sugar. Fold the cream into the yogurt.

3 Spoon the berries into 4 ramekins and put the yogurt mixture on top.

Try using other fruits, too.

4 Sprinkle on the turbinado sugar; put the brûlées in the freezer for 15 minutes. Heat the broiler to high. Broil as close as possible to the heat until the sugar has melted.

Cool slightly before serving so the sugar forms a crisp crust.

Chicken Pitas with Yogurt & Mint Dressing

This is a mildly spicy dish with a refreshing, cooling minty sauce. Serve in pita breads for a light lunch or dinner.

You will need:

For the chicken
- 4 tbsp plain yogurt
- 1 tsp mild curry paste
- 1 tsp honey
- 1 tsp lemon juice
- 3 chicken "tenders"

For the sauce
- 4 tbsp plain yogurt
- 1 tsp lemon juice
- pinch of salt
- 8 mint leaves

To serve
- 4 small pita breads
- 1 small head green lettuce

Makes 4

☆Annabel's Tip
Make sure you wash your hands after handling raw chicken. And check that it is cooked all the way through before serving.

Serve while the chicken is still warm.

Mix

Snip

1 First put the yogurt, curry paste, honey, and lemon juice in a bowl and mix together. Add the chicken and mix to coat. Cover and leave to marinate for 30 minutes (or overnight in the fridge).

2 Meanwhile, make the sauce: put the yogurt, lemon juice, and salt into a bowl. Roll the mint leaves into a cylinder and use scissors to snip into little ribbons. Mix everything together and keep in the fridge until needed.

Grill

Fill

3 Preheat the broiler to low. Put the chicken on a lined baking sheet. Spoon over half the marinade left in the bowl and broil for 6 minutes. Turn the chicken over, spoon on the remaining marinade, and broil for 6 minutes or until cooked.

4 Warm the pitas in the oven so they puff up. As soon as they are cool enough to handle, split them open and fill with the lettuce leaves, chicken, and yogurt dressing. Then serve.

Index

Annabel Karmel

Annabel is a mother of three and best-selling author on cooking for children. She has written 16 successful books that are sold all over the world.

She is an expert in devising tasty and nutritious meals for children without the need to spend hours in the kitchen.

Annabel is a leading UK expert on children's nutritional needs and has created a popular range of Children's food in supermarkets in the UK. She travels frequently to the US and has appeared on the *Today Show*, *Live with Regis and Kelly*, and *The View*.

Annabel was awarded an MBE in 2006 in the Queen's Honours List for her outstanding work in the field of child nutrition.

Other children's titles written by Annabel
The Toddler Cookbook 978-0-75663-505-3
Mom and Me Cookbook 978-0-75661-006-7

For recipes and advice
visit Annabel's website at
www.annabelkarmel.com

Acknowledgments

With thanks from Annabel to: Valerie Berry, Rachael Foster, Dave King, Mary Ling, and Caroline Stearns for their help in making this book. **And thanks to the children who appeared in the photographs:** Ruby Christian-Muldoon, Luella Disley, Sonny Edwards, Meganne Galivo, Lewis Matton, Ethan Michaels, Dominic Mosca, Samuel Phelps-Jones, Molly Saunders, Jaden Stauch, Chloe Tingle, James Watson, Brian Wong, and Natalya Wright. **Thanks also to:** Katie Giovanni, Seiko Hatfield, and Beth Hester.

Picture Credits: The publisher would like to thank the following for their kind permission to reproduce their photographs:
(Key: a-above; b-below/bottom; c-center; f-far; l-left; r-right; t-top)
Alamy Images: Balfour Studios 30ftl; Ricardo Beliel / BrazilPhotos 40tr; Blickwinkel / Schmidbauer 4fbr; Adam Burton 44t; Nigel Cattlin 14tr, 30tl; Central America 22bl, 22tr; Dennis Cox 18tr; Foodfolio 5bl, 36fbr; Andrew Fox 26cl; Paolo Gallo 10fcra; Mark Gibson 30tr; Greenshoots Communications 40tl; Tim Hill / Cephas Picture Library 5ftl; Wayne Hutchinson 14tl; James Clarke Images 10t; Dennis MacDonald 36tl; Ian McKinnell 18tc; Photography 1st 22tc; Ingo Schulz / Imagebroker 36fbl; Martin Shields 22clb; Jason Smalley / Wildscape 36ftl; Eric Tormey 30ftr; Maximilian Weinzierl 4bl; Andrew Woodley 4fbl; Russell Young / Danita Delimont 36tr. **Corbis**: Ted Horowitz 36fclb. **Getty Images**: DAJ 26tc; Johner Images 6tc; Nordic Photos / Jerker Andersson 36ftr; Photographer's Choice / Ian O'Leary 26tr; Science Faction / Ed Darack 6tl; StockFood Creative / Lew Robertson 36bc; Tim Graham Photo Library 14tc; Win-Initiative 6tr. **Photolibrary**: 40tc; Digital Vision 40tc; Akira Kaede 18tl. **StockFood.com**: Susie M. Eising 40br; Bernd Euler 40fcl; FoodPhotogr. Eising 26tl; Studio Schiermann 22cb.
All other images © Dorling Kindersley. For further information see: **www.dkimages.com**